AUTO ACCIDENT

— LAW IN —

SOUTH DAKOTA AND IOWA

David J. King, Esq.

Jacobs & Whitehall
21750 Hardy Oak Blvd
Suite 104
#51700
San Antonio, Texas 78258
www.jacobsandwhitehall.com

Ordering Information:

Quantity sales. Special discounts are available on quantity purchases by corporations, associations, and others. For details, contact the publisher at the address above.

Orders by U.S. trade bookstores and wholesalers, please contact Jacobs & Whitehall: Tel: (888) 991-2766 or visit www.jacobsandwhitehall.com.

Printed in the United States of America

Published in 2021

ISBN: 978-1-954506-34-3

PREFACE

David J. King is shareholder and founding member of King Law Firm, P.C. He received his undergraduate and law degrees from the University of South Dakota. David is a member of the American Bar Association, the American Association for Justice, the Iowa Association for Justice, the Iowa State Bar Association, the South Dakota Trial Lawyers Associations, National Organization of Social Security Claimant Representative, the Top 100 Lawyers, and Who's Who Top Lawyer. He specializes in representing people injured in automobile accidents, worker's compensation cases, insurance claims, and disability matters.

DEDICATION

This book is dedicated to all those people who have suffered an injury, in an automobile accident, a worker's compensation injury, or who have made an insurance claim or a disability claim. I respect and admire their strength to stand up to a system that frequently tries to wear them down.

DISCLAIMER

This publication is intended to be used for educational purposes only. No legal advice is being given, and no attorney-client relationship is intended to be created by reading this material. The author assumes no liability for any errors or omissions, how this book or its contents are used or interpreted, or for any consequences resulting directly or indirectly from the use of this book. For legal or any other advice, please consult an experienced attorney or the appropriate expert who is aware of the specific facts of your case and is knowledgeable in the law in your jurisdiction.

King Law Firm, P.C.
101 N. Phillips Avenue
Suite 602
Sioux Falls, SD 57104
(605) 332 4000
www.davidkinglawfirm.com

Testimonials

"I am so thankful for you! I don't know why you chose to sacrifice so much of your time & energy on me, but I'm so glad you did! You truly are a Man of God… one that's not afraid to get his hands a little dirty. Just like Jesus; He hung out with the same people you do David: the accused, the criminals, the poor. You will always be in my prayers; that the Lord deeply blesses you + keeps you. That he gives his angels charge over you + your family, lest you dash your foot against a stone. I just don't think you even know the enormity of what you did for me…for us… for my family. For one, we can actually enjoy Easter this year now. But really, it's just so much more. They haven't invented a word to tell you how grateful I am. God Bless you, David. Thank you so, so, so, much!

– *Liz W.*

****

"I wanted to reach out and thank you for everything you have done to help me with my lawsuit. I always felt you had my best interest and what I needed to do for my health. I truly appreciate that. You're a good person. Thanks for that. Sometimes people lose why they do what they do. Never once felt that with you. From the bottom of my heart, thank you!!!"

– *K. Behnke*

****

"Mr. King is the most responsible, caring, honest, and professional attorney we've worked with on my son's case. I feel he really cares and is doing his best for our welfare. I'd refer him to my best friend if they needed a good attorney."

– S. Ruth

****

"David King has gone above and beyond to assist in an insurance claim I had. I felt 100% effort from my lawyer David King while going through my case. I know David King has my daughter's and my best interest in mind!"

– T. Dannelley

****

"I would highly recommend King Law Firm. No problems with them whatsoever. Very courteous and professional and always made me feel comfortable."

– Recent Client

****

"I am very happy with the help I had. I will tell others they treated me and other people great here. Everyone was very kind. The process was a little long, but it was definitely worth it."

– M. M.

****

TABLE OF CONTENTS

About The Author

The King Law Firm has helped thousands of clients and their families in auto accidents. After reaching a fair settlement, clients can heal and move on with their lives without the financial burden caused by a serious accident.

Key Takeaways:

- Attorney David King is an attorney you can trust to fight for your interests and obtain fair compensation for your injuries.
- Over 30 years of experience handling auto insurance accident claims and lawsuits have

resulted in the King Law Firm recovering over $100 million in damages.

- The King Law Firm's proven, streamlined approach to handling auto accident injury cases increases recovery of damages compared to self-representation.
- Insurance companies are not on your side. Without the representation of an experienced auto accident attorney, you will not reach a fair settlement.

Attorney-Client Relationship – Building Trust

When I first meet clients after they have been in an accident, I hear a lot of concerns about medical bills. They are worried about how they are going to pay for medical treatment. They have questions about who will pay for their medical treatment and about getting their car fixed.

I also hear a lot of concerns about how the accident is affecting the entire family financially. They are worried about how they will pay the bills during the pendency of their case.

In those first few meetings with a client, I work to build their trust by trying to understand their injuries and how they are affecting them. We take the time to work up their case from the start, leaving nothing out.

We start by listening to the client's story and how their injuries have affected them. Then we record the information we need, meet with witnesses, and, if required, hire private investigators. We work the case up properly, documenting the many different types of injuries they have sustained – economic, physical, and mental/ emotional.

The economic injuries are easier to itemize and prove and include damages like medical bills and lost wages. However, in my view, the non-economic damages are even more critical to work-up and prove, such as:

- the permanency of the injury;
- the nature and extent of the injury;
- the effect on the person's mind, body, and spirit;
- their loss of enjoyment of life; and
- their pain and suffering.

These types of damages matter greatly. We've been working on auto accident cases for a long time, and we do an outstanding job at it.

When we first meet with a client, we begin collecting the necessary evidence:

- Documentation received from the police
- Insurance exchange information
- Documentation from the at-fault insurance carrier
- Correspondence from their insurance carrier
- Driver's license and health insurance information

Then we have them execute a variety of authorizations to gather their medical records:

- HIPAA authorizations
- HITECH medical authorizations
- Release of insurance information
- Medicare authorizations and proof of representation to Medicare

We need all this information to process their claim adequately.

It's critical to the attorney-client relationship for a client to meet with their lawyer and establish a relationship of trust. I often hear that lawyers don't meet with their clients. That's certainly not how we do it at King Law Firm.

At King Law Firm, we have a streamlined process to professionally work up and resolve cases. Once we've established that attorney-client relationship, we set up follow-up appointments. We have internal case processing standards, whereby we handle the case on a reliable timeline. Following this process is essential to move each case forward successfully.

Why I Wrote This Book?

I want the readers to better understand their rights, and responsibilities, what they can expect in an auto accident case, how long it can take, and the proper legal handling of an auto accident case.

CHAPTER 1

IMMEDIATE STEPS TO TAKE AFTER AN AUTO ACCIDENT

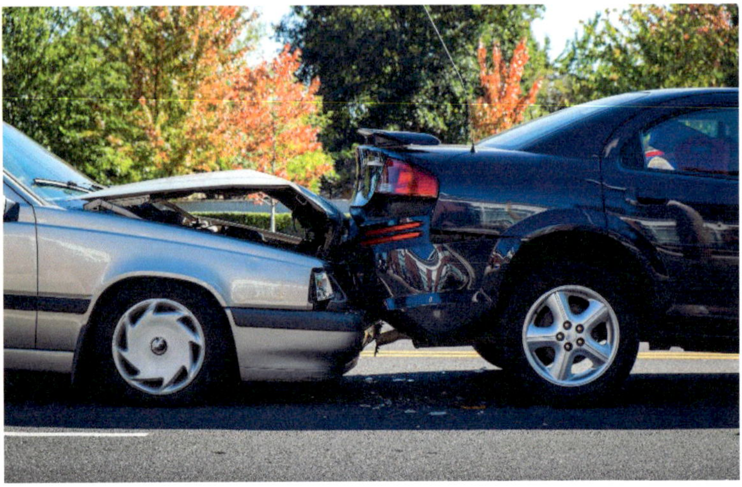

When you've been in an auto accident you need to pull your car over to a safe spot, if possible, so another person doesn't come along and hit you again. My advice would be to not move the car from the scene of the accident unless absolutely necessary and wait until the police arrive. You don't want to interfere with the officer's investigation.

If you're able, take pictures of your car and the damage to the other party's car and license plate. It would be best if you told the police completely what happened and why the accident occurred so that they can do an adequate investigation and cite the other side.

You also need to get the medical treatment you need. Frequently that means a trip to the emergency room to start and follow-up appointments with the family doctor, physical therapist, chiropractor, orthopedic surgeon, or neurosurgeon if the injuries require it.

Before you give a statement to the insurance company or fill out their paperwork, you should talk to an experienced attorney that has handled many car accident cases. There is no substitute for experience.

The insurance company has thousands of employees who often take incomplete statements or statements taken out-of-context that will more than likely be used against you later. I would recommend getting an attorney involved sooner rather than later, and definitely <u>before</u> you ever give a statement to the insurance company.

Medical Attention

It is very important to seek medical attention after an accident. One of the main issues in an auto accident case is the nature and extent of the injuries. It takes expert medical evidence, and opinion evidence, generally obtained from a doctor, to demonstrate this. You must be very clear about what happened when you see a physician, whether in the emergency room, family doctor, physical therapist, chiropractor, or mental health professional. My advice is to be very clear with each and every doctor regarding all of the symptoms you experience every time you're in the physician's office to make it easier to prove all the injuries you have suffered because of the accident.

Building A Strong Case

In building a strong case, some of the most critical evidence from the scene of the accident include:

- 911 call recording (we obtain and transcribe)
- Insurance exchange of information
- Police or highway patrol's report

- Physical evidence

Sometimes the visible damage to the car indicates the amount of damage that the human being(s) inside suffered, but frequently that's not the case. It's not uncommon for the property damage to not look all that bad, but the injuries sustained by the occupants will be very significant.

Sometimes, people at the accident scene may not realize they've been hurt or the full extent of their injuries. It's easy to overlook when you have adrenaline flowing or from the shock of the accident. It's only in the days and weeks, perhaps months to come, that the true nature of your injuries comes to light.

At that stage, we help our clients by documenting everything along the way, in terms of medical damages, physical damages, and non-economic damages. We can hire expert witnesses if needed, such as accident reconstructionists or doctors specializing in impairment ratings and functional capacities assessments; specialists can evaluate and treat the actual injury the client has sustained.

Sometimes a family doctor isn't suited to that type of treatment. We walk them through all aspects of their injury case, beginning to end.

Liability & Fault

Even with accidents that are clearly the other driver's fault, it is still wise to work with an experienced personal injury attorney with extensive experience in auto accident claims. The insurance company is still often simply not going to treat you fairly. For instance, they will claim you're not that hurt or had pre-existing injuries. They will want you to execute medical authorizations to turn your medical records over to them, and then they will try to use the medical records against you.

It's not enough just that liability is certain. You need an attorney on your side who understands how to deal with your injuries. One who has experience in getting the right doctors' opinions and who has experience working against the "pre-existing conditions" defense and the "you're not really injured" defense. Most of our cases are where liability is certain, and our clients have benefited from having an attorney to represent them against the insurance companies.

If you are partially at fault for the accident, it will impact your case. South Dakota has "contributory negligence," meaning there can be negligence assigned on the part of the plaintiff. South Dakota Codified Law (SDCL) § 20-9-2 states that when a plaintiff's contributory negligence is more than "slight," in comparison to the defendant's negligence, it acts as a barrier to any recovery of damages. The term "slight" is defined as small compared with the defendant's negligence. However, suppose the plaintiff's contributory negligence is not more than slight. In that case, the plaintiff can still recover damages, but the amount recovered is reduced in proportion to the amount of their contributory negligence. South Dakota law is very complex on the issue of contributory negligence. It can trip up a good claim, which is another reason to get an experienced lawyer working on your case right away.

Iowa has a "comparative fault" statute. Iowa Code Chapter 668. Under Iowa's comparative fault law, the jury determines the fault between the parties to the lawsuit. Once the relative fault of both parties is determined, the plaintiff's recovery is reduced by the amount of their attributed portion of their fault or negligence.

CHAPTER 2

FILING A PERSONAL INJURY CLAIM

In South Dakota, the general statute of limitations for a personal injury action is three years, SDCL §15-2-14, whereas, in Iowa, it is only two years. Iowa Code §614.1(2). There are other timeframes to consider as well.

For instance, in South Dakota, if you are injured by someone in an official government role, for example, you are rear-ended by a city or state-owned vehicle, you would first have to give the government authority notice within 180 days of the accident, SDCL §3-21-2 then you would have only two years to bring your car accident case. Statutes of limitations differ by jurisdiction and can be very complex. It's vital to get an experienced lawyer involved early so as to not bar a claim by waiting too long.

Client Expectations

Once you secure representation and file a claim, you should expect your case to be worked up appropriately. An experienced attorney should put together medical evidence, and have it examined by a doctor specializing in the related medical area to determine whether the injury is permanent or transitory.

You should expect a period of negotiation with the insurance company. We try to give the insurance company every opportunity to settle the case reasonably without a lawsuit. Unfortunately, with many insurance companies, they seem to be no longer be interested in settling a case reasonably. So frequently, that means we will have to file a lawsuit.

Filing a lawsuit does not mean that your case will necessarily go to trial. When you file a lawsuit, the legal paperwork will be filed with the court by our office. Interrogatories typically follow that with a request for the production of documents, depositions, and medical evidence worked up.

Personal Injury Settlement

Generally, there are two types of damages in a personal injury case. The first would be economic damages, and the second would be non-economic damages. Economic damages include:

- Cost of medical bills
- Wage loss
- Time off-work
- Pre-judgment interest
- Loss of future earnings
- Ongoing medical treatments
- Property damage

Many economic damages can easily be measured, but a lot of non-economic damages need to be considered as well, such as pain, discomfort, suffering, and disfigurement.

Past costs, expenses, and damages are relatively straightforward to document and calculate an amount and prove. The amount of property damage suffered to the car, wage loss, medical bills, and pre-judgment interest can be calculated from the proper documentation. However, consider the action of any *future* medical care and other expenses that may need to be projected to the end of the injured party's life.

Projections should be compiled with the use of expert witnesses. Suppose there will be future medical expenses, such as MRIs, injections, surgery, or medication. In that case, we need to establish the cost of those necessary treatments and establish the frequency they are anticipated to be needed. We need to project these costs out throughout a person's expected lifetime.

Having an experienced personal injury attorney to represent you can increase your likelihood of a more significant settlement. I've had cases where an insurance adjuster has been at the victim's door the day after an accident with a check in hand, offering a settlement of $2,500 - $5,000. However, after my firm has properly worked up the case we have settled the case later for $250,000-$500,000.

Having an experienced attorney dramatically increases the likelihood of a better outcome for the client in terms of a settlement. Frequently, the injured person has little experience in negotiating, not to mention valuing and resolving those types of claims. These are things we do every day in my office, multiple times a day. We have the contacts, reputation, and staff to put everything together and help the client and their family reach a better outcome.

CHAPTER 3

INSURANCE CLAIMS AND COVERAGE

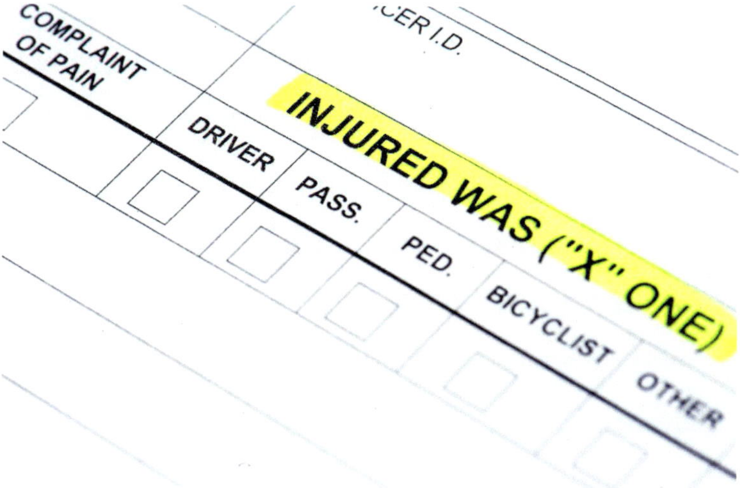

People will often believe they have "full coverage" when discussing auto insurance. However, they don't fully understand what that means most of the time. When someone says they have "full coverage," they usually have at least liability insurance coverage. Frequently, full coverage also means:

- Medical payments coverage (applies without regard to any fault)

- Comprehensive coverage (applies if you are at fault or your car is damaged without an accident, as in a force of nature)
- Underinsured and uninsured motorist coverage

Medical payments coverage applies without regard to who's at fault and covers the cost of medical treatment up to the limits of that coverage under the policy. Comprehensive coverage applies if your car is damaged, and that coverage would also apply to the at-fault driver's property damage under their insurance policy.

Often, people don't know the full range of benefits they may have available to them under their own automobile insurance policy. When they believe they have "full coverage," there are coverages that are not included, such as rental car coverage or death and dismemberment coverage.

Many people only have liability coverage on their cars. They may think their car isn't worth much, so they just have liability coverage. In my opinion, this is a mistake a big mistake. Liability insurance coverage only applies and provides benefits to someone else that you would injure in an accident you were at fault for. Other types of automobile insurance coverage, such as collision, medical payments, uninsured and underinsured motorist benefits, death and dismemberment, and rental car coverage, provide benefits to the insured that can be very important automobile insurance coverage to fully compensate one for all of their loses in an automobile collision.

Typically, state laws *require* fairly minimal basic liability insurance coverage. In South Dakota, $25,000 in liability coverage is required SDCL §32-35-70. In Iowa, only $20,000 of liability insurance is required. Iowa Codified law §321A.1. Many years ago, the state minimums were set and haven't kept up with inflation. Often, people need more coverage than just the liability alone. We recommend that people obtain more bare minimum liability insurance coverage.

The uninsured and underinsured motorist provision coverage, as well as medical payments coverage, is very inexpensive. Those benefits should be maintained at levels well over the state minimum. I recommend most people have a minimum of $100,000 in liability and uninsured or underinsured motorist coverage and a minimum of $5,000 in medical payments coverage.

Although liability insurance is required under South Dakota and Iowa law, people often let their insurance coverage lapse. Therefore, the uninsured or underinsured provisions of your insurance coverage are what will protect <u>you</u> when you are injured by the negligence of that uninsured or underinsured driver. When you make an uninsured or underinsured motorist claim, your insurance company must follow certain claim management practices, one of which requires it to fairly value the claim. And to properly document the claim. You have contracted for this insurance coverage with them, and it's important they honor their contractual commitment to their insureds.

Too often, insurance companies don't honor their responsibilities to their clients. Insurance companies tend to delay, deny, or defend the claim.

Their concern is not you; their concern is solely about money. They want to evaluate the claim for the absolute minimum they can force somebody to accept on a claim. They don't care about the injured person. They don't care about their family or how it's affected them. They want to be "released from liability" as soon as possible, for as little as possible.

In underinsured cases, it's vital to have an attorney involved who is experienced in dealing with these technical matters. The policies are complex, and you could end up barring yourself from recovering damages without the experience of an attorney knowledgeable in these areas.

When you look at the costs of the standard auto insurance premium, most of the automobile insurance premium is the cost of the liability coverage, then the comprehensive and collision coverage. These are essential insurance coverage, but neither one protects you in an accident. The type of coverage that will protect the person's interest in the accident is the uninsured or underinsured motorist and medical payments coverage.

Medical payments coverage, in some states referred to as personal injury protection (PIP), is a first-dollar coverage, meaning you don't have to meet a co-pay or deductible to receive the benefit. You have options under that coverage that you might not under a typical health insurance policy. It is coverage that is available for anyone in your car with permission. Having medical payments coverage gives peace of mind, knowing that when there is a car full of kids or friends in an automobile, there would be medical coverage available for all of them if there was a bad accident.

The average cost of medical treatments for someone who has been injured in an auto accident can vary. For instance, you could expect to see between $10,000 and $30,000 in medical bills for common whiplash in a rear-end auto collision. We also frequently see surgical cases where someone needs a cervical fusion or lumbar fusion, and the cost can get well into the six figures.

CHAPTER 4

DEALING WITH THE AT-FAULT PARTY'S INSURANCE

The at-fault party's insurance company will want to reach out to you right away when they first learn of the accident. They will try to get a statement from you over the phone. I would recommend that you don't give a statement to an insurance company without first hiring an auto accident lawyer. The insurance company can learn the essential facts of the accident directly from the police report.

Too often, insurance adjusters will go to an injured person's hospital room or call them as they are just out of the ER. People in these conditions should not be giving statements to overzealous insurance adjusters. Frequently, they are medicated and have just been through a traumatic event; it's the wrong time and place to provide such an important thing as a statement. Often people don't know how badly they are hurt in the immediate aftermath of an automobile accident. When you give a recorded statement, the adjuster may attempt to put "words in your mouth" or attempt to construe facts in a certain way that can hurt your case. It's very dangerous in an automobile collision case. Proceed with caution!

To protect our clients, our firm will prevent that from happening. We get a letter of representation out to the insurance company and advise them that our client will not be giving a statement to the insurance company. It's not going to happen without our presence. We need to be there to protect their interests.

You don't have to answer any of their questions. The claims adjuster may be calling you repeatedly, trying to get a statement. It's important to them because they want to take anything you say, any potential slip-up you make, and use it against you in a court of law. In a criminal case, the police must notify you of your *Miranda* rights anything you say can and will be used against you in a court of law. In the civil context, the insurance company doesn't have to warn you that they will use any statement you make against you, but that's exactly what they want to do.

They want to take a statement from you when you're unprepared, minimize any liability on their insured's part and minimize their risk of exposure on the claim. In no way, shape, or form are they looking out for your interests. They are looking out for the insurance company's interest.

Generally, with your own insurance company you have a "duty of cooperation"; written in your insurance policy. But with someone else's insurance company, you don't have to cooperate with them. You should only work with them through an experienced automobile accident attorney.

The at-fault party's insurance company will frequently use the following three tactics to avoid paying out timely on a claim or denying the claim altogether:

Delay. One of the insurance company's main tactics is to delay the case and delay payment. People are often out of work, their medical bills, deductibles, and co-pays are mounting, and their pain and suffering aren't stopping. Often, the insurance company will delay processing the claim to take economic advantage of the person injured in the automobile accident to leverage the injured party's financial condition to secure a settlement favorable to the insurance company.

Deny the claim. Another tactic used by insurance companies is to deny the claim by asserting or arguing that you were "contributorily" or "comparatively" negligent, meaning your actions partially caused the accident. Those defenses, if established, may reduce your recovery or bar you from recovering damages at all. The insurance company may also say you have "assumed the risk" of the injury or come up with a similar legal defense.

Insurance companies may also argue that your claim is barred by the statute of limitations or notice provisions. If you wait too long to give notice or file and serve your lawsuit, your case may be barred due to the statute of limitation. You have no rights after the statute of limitations has passed. Therefore, you don't want to sit back and let them develop those defenses. They will also use defenses such as failure to mitigate damages, meaning you should have sought additional medical care, but you didn't. It is a weak defense, but it is used all the time.

They will also try to argue the injured person may have pre-existing conditions or that the injury in this accident wasn't very bad. They will claim you already had a bad back or neck. They will hire doctors, nurses, lawyers, and adjusters to pore over all those prior records with a fine-tooth comb to prove their defenses.

Defend. Another tactic frequently used by insurance companies is forcing you into the litigation process. They don't want to settle the case fairly with you. They want to force you to file a lawsuit. They want to force your claim to be delayed and force you to increase the expenses you are forced to incur to recover your claim fairly.

In my 30 years of professional practice, I've seen a change in their claims handling nationwide. Insurance companies are getting tougher on claims. You need to have a lawyer who has been there before. You need a lawyer who has successfully handled these cases in front of juries and to the Supreme Court and won. You need an attorney who will force the automobile insurance company to pay what the claim is worth. You need to have an attorney the insurance companies respect. My advice to clients often is to stand up for themselves, not cut and run but rather stay and fight. It is the harder way, but it is often the right way to maximize their recovery, not only for them but also for their family.

CHAPTER 5

HAVING THE KING LAW FIRM ON YOUR SIDE

If you try to go it alone, the insurance company will try to take advantage of your inexperience. We frequently see people hurt their cases by trying to handle them themselves. When we're involved, the resolutions are very different. We've worked with and beaten every insurance company in this area. We have a solid record of success. Our legal expertise usually results in positive outcomes for our clients and their families. Financially, it will help the client and their family. Our firm will take care of all of the paperwork you need to properly process your claim and maximize your recovery.

By using our contacts and connections in the legal and medical community, we help our clients protect themselves against the defense tactics of the insurance companies. We work with experts throughout South Dakota and Iowa every day:

- We meet with the doctors to secure their opinions, having them identify the injuries our clients have suffered and the cause of those injuries.
- We hire vocational experts.
- We hire physical therapists for functional capacities assessments.
- We work with specialized doctors for impairment ratings.
- We pursue rehabilitation claims.

We make sure that all the proof is sufficient to satisfy the proper legal standard to prove the claim, and we ensure the insurance company is aware of it.

When I meet with clients, I look them in the eye. They are not going to wonder where their case is at or what is going on. We set follow-up appointments. We want clients to bring in any questions or concerns they have. Here, you're like family, and we treat you that way. For instance, maybe they have an unpaid medical bill that has been ignored, and they are getting pressured to pay those outstanding medical bills. I want them to bring it to the office because we can often help recover those bills. We try to have a very good rapport with our clients. We regularly meet with them and their family members to hear their whole stories. To learn how the accident has affected the entire family.

Thousands of people have trusted us to represent them on their personal injury cases for over 30 years. We have recovered untold millions of dollars in auto accident recoveries. We have a well-known history of respect in the legal community and for caring for our clients. Through online reviews and social media, many clients have publicly declared what we've done for them. We know how an injury claim can impact the injured person and their whole family, and we don't take that responsibility lightly. We take getting to know the client and their story very seriously. By getting to know what really happened, and how it affects them in all aspects of their lives, we can effectively present their case to the insurance company, the jury, or the court.

I have a framed letter that I received decades ago from a client. It talks about everything I did for him and his family. Several other lawyers had rejected him before seeing me on his case. We won that claim. The letter is tearful, talking about how I was able to put clothes on his children's backs and how I was able to help their family financially. They felt respected and vindicated, and I cherish that client. It is a serious responsibility to represent a client in an automobile accident case. We take that we are responsible very seriously.

This letter isn't the only one. I have several framed letters at my office just like it. They are glowing reviews thanking us for everything we did for them and caring about them. You can look at our public testimonials on our website or our five-star Google reviews and Facebook reviews to see we are very well-respected.

Every day we look at this as a responsibility to earn our clients' trust and respect. We look at it as an honor to represent them and be entrusted with their family's situation.

I have been awarded virtually every award out there:

- American Institute of Personal Injury Law Firms 2021
- America's Most Honored Professions Top 10%
- Great Plains Super Lawyers – 2018 to 2021
- Lawyers of Distinction – Excellence in Personal Injury Law
- Lead Counsel Rating – Workmen's Compensation Law
- Top 100 Trial Lawyers
- Top 10 Personal Injury Lawyers in South Dakota
- Top 100 Registry - 2020 Attorney of the Year
- Workers' Injury Law & Advocacy Group – The Nation's top Injured Worker Attorney (2018)

In addition to the numerous awards and accolades I have received, I was honored to serve as a law clerk for the Chief Justice of the South Dakota Supreme Court. This was a very high honor coming out of law school. I was also honored to be an Adjunct Professor of Law at the University of South Dakota, where I taught Insurance Law. I have been honored to be published in the *South Dakota Law Review.* We are very proud of the work we are doing, and we take the responsibility of zealously representing our clients very seriously.

INDEX

P

S

U

V

Notes

Made in United States
Troutdale, OR
10/01/2026

55032811R00029